MRYAH
7/10

D1283121

HOW?D THEY DO THAT?

in...

THE AZTEC EMPIRE

Mitchell Lane
PUBLISHERS
P.O. Box 196
Hockessin, Delaware 19707

Ancient Egypt

Ancient Greece

Ancient Mesopotamia

Ancient Rome

 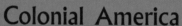The Aztec Empire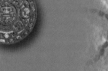

Colonial America

Elizabethan England

The Mayan Civilization

The Persian Empire

Pre-Columbian America

Coxitipan

Xiuhcoac

TOTOTEPEC

Tzintzuntza

Patzcuaro

Tlatlauh

Cihua

inchan Ah

aixtlahuacar

llantonco

Te

Te

Hua

Nopallar

TOTOTEPE

PACIF

Maximum extension of the Aztec Empire

Enclaves with unclear status or mostly uninhabited

Disputed areas (1500 - 1519)

Trade routes (hypothetical alignment)

HOW?'D THEY DO THAT?

in...

THE AZTEC EMPIRE

GULF OF MEXICO

chpan

epec

Cuetlaxtlan

apan

an

Tochtepec

COATZACUALCO

olollan

cac

Mictlan

Tzinacantlan

Tehuantepec

WILLIAM NOBLE

N

OCEAN

Xoconochco

PUBLISHERS

Printing   1   2   3   4   5   6   7   8   9

Library of Congress Cataloging-in-Publication Data
Noble, William.
  How'd they do that in the Aztec Empire / by William Noble.
      p. cm. — (How'd they do that?)
  Includes bibliographical references and index.
  ISBN 978-1-58415-824-0 (library bound)
  1.Aztecs—Juvenile literature. I. Title.
  F1219.73.N635 2009
  972'.018–dc22

                                                            2009001301

PUBLISHER'S NOTE: This story is based on the author's extensive research, which he believes to be accurate. Documentation of such research is contained on page 60.

To reflect current usage, we have chosen to use the secular era designations BCE ("before the common era") and CE ("of the common era") instead of the traditional designations BC ("before Christ") and AD (*anno Domini,* "in the year of the Lord").

The internet sites referenced herein were active as of the publication date. Due to the fleeting nature of some web sites, we cannot guarantee they will all be active when you are reading this book.

PLB

CONTENTS

The night was cloudless, and the stars sparkled above the darkened Valley of Mexico. The Aztec priests had gathered at the summit of Citlaltépec, a high peak known as the Hill of Stars, not far outside the capital city of Tenochtitlán. Once every fifty-two years on this special night, the high priests searched the darkened heavens for favorable signs and pled with their gods to allow the sun to appear with the coming dawn. If their pleas went unheard, and the sun never came, they were sure the world would end.

Nearby, and guarded by the priests, was a young warrior captured in a recent battle and prepared for sacrifice. The warrior stood quietly, his head heavily plumed with feathers, his arms sporting silver amulets, his thick, strong chest bare. He had been specially chosen by the

THE "NEW FIRE" CEREMONY

emperor because the Aztec gods favored the bravest, handsomest sacrifice victims.

Over the past twelve days, according to Aztec custom, all fires throughout the empire had been put out. All furniture had been thrown away. All statues of the gods had been tossed in the water. All homes, patios, and walkways had been swept clean.

By dusk, the early evening shadows had crept over the land. Throughout the day, men, women, and children had climbed to the roofs of their houses to gain a clear view of the heavens. When the curtain of night descended, as they looked where there would normally have been fires, they saw only blackness and hope.

On the Hill of Stars, the head priest readied himself. He wore dark, somber clothes and a black cloak to match his jet black hair, which was long and thick and matted with dried blood. His skin showed many scars and blemishes from almost daily bloodletting. Most noticeably, his black eyes gleamed with purpose and certainty. If he performed the sacrifice properly and well, and if the sacrifice was met by favorable signs in the heavens, the sun would rise with the dawn, and the Aztec Empire would begin a new fifty-two year life cycle.

But if there were no favorable signs in the heavens, and the sun failed to appear, the Aztec Empire—and the world—would be doomed.

What the priests sought in the night sky were the stars that made up the constellation Pleiades. They knew the brightest stars in this constellation could be easily seen on a clear night, and that Aztec ances-tors had followed the Pleiades' path through the sky fifty-two years earlier . . . and fifty-two years before that . . . and fifty-two years before that. They also knew that the constellation "traveled" across the heavens, with its stars moving in the same direction at the same time. The Ple-iades went up and up, then reached its highest point. If the gods favored the Aztecs' sacrifice, the Pleiades would then start to go down and down as the night wore on.

On this night, there was a shout from the head priest, who pointed at a faraway cluster of lights in the dark sky. He gathered his fellow priests, and they watched as the star cluster—certain now it was the Pleiades—inched higher and higher.

The Pleiades reached its highest point . . . and suddenly the con-stellation began to descend again. The priests knew the sign: The movement of the heavens had not stopped. The gods were pleased.

A sculpture from 1500 CE representing a xiuhmolpilli ("year bundle"), or fifty-two-year cycle

During the Aztec New Fire ceremony, 52 bundles of reeds were burned. The ceremony also included human sacrifice and the lighting of fires across the Empire. It marked the start of a new 52-year cycle in the Aztec calendar.

The high priest ordered the sacrifice victim readied, and with priests holding his arms and legs and stretching him on a flat stone, the high priest lit a small fire, then cut out the victim's heart and threw it on the flame. The high priest made a new fire in the victim's open chest. Another priest lit a torch from it and passed the new fire to messengers waiting with other torches. Their torches would be lit with the new fire.

The messengers, carrying their torches, went from home to home across the countryside, lighting fires where people had put them out. Within hours, the Aztec Empire was ablaze with "new fire." It would be another fifty-two years before these fires were extinguished.

Huitzilopochtli, the Aztec god of war, was also the god of the sun. The Aztecs offered him hearts of their sacrifice victims so that their world would not plunge into darkness.

WHO WERE THE AZTECS?

Chapter 1

In the early fourteenth century, a weary group of travelers came upon a rattlesnake-infested swampy lake in the middle of what would eventually be called the Valley of Mexico. They were a nomadic people, and they had been wandering for hundreds of years in search of a sign that would mark their permanent home. Huitzilopochtli, their god of war, had told them to keep searching until they came upon an eagle with a rattlesnake in its claws, perched on a cactus.

As the travelers examined this new place, they spotted an eagle. It had a rattlesnake in its talons, and it was perched on top of a cactus. They had found their new home. In time, it would become the seat of a fabulous empire.

For many generations, they had worked for other people, usually as vassals or mercenaries, paying tribute and following orders. They were often disliked and sometimes feared but never encouraged to settle or stay.

So they had wandered. Their myths and legends told them they had come from the north, from Aztlán, many centuries before. They were a warlike people, short, stocky, with flat faces and prominent noses. And their gods demanded blood worship. We know them now as Aztecs.

The strands that formed the Aztec culture go back thousands of years to the Olmecs, people who lived in the lowland, tropical areas of what is now south-central Mexico. The Olmecs flourished from 1200 to 400 BCE and, like the Aztecs, practiced a form of bloodletting with stingray spikes and maguey (cactus) thorns to appease their gods. There's no evidence, however, that they also performed human sacrifice. In the Nahuatl language (which both the Olmecs and the Aztecs spoke), *Olmec* means "rubber people." It's clear the Olmecs developed rubber balls, which became part of an unusual ballgame that without major change was played by the Aztecs two thousand years later (see Chapter Four).

Several hundred years after the Olmecs, a new culture developed in the eastern portion of Mexico: the Yucatán. There the Mayans thrived, and their civilization touched the edges of what was to become the Valley of Mexico, where the Aztecs would arise. The Mayans, who

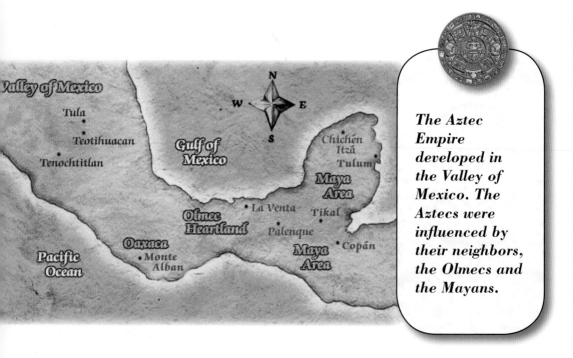

Valley of Mexico

Tula

Teotihuacan

Tenochtitlan

Pacific Ocean

Oaxaca
• Monte Alban

Gulf of Mexico

Olmec Heartland

• La Venta

Palenque

Chichén Itzá

Tulum

Maya Area

Tikal

Copán

Maya Area

N   W   E   S

The Aztec Empire developed in the Valley of Mexico. The Aztecs were influenced by their neighbors, the Olmecs and the Mayans.

flourished from about 300 CE to 900 CE, developed a type of communication using picture-drawing rather than words. These drawings are known as glyphs, and in the Mayan culture they could be quite elaborate. They could be read just as one might read a book today. They contained symbols, human figures, animals, and other items from nature. They could tell a story or describe an event.

Hundreds of years after the Mayans, the Aztecs developed their own pictographs. In fact, the Aztec glyphs are the major source for understanding the Aztec culture. The similarities between the Mayan glyphs and the Aztec glyphs are striking.

According to religious historians David Carrasco and Scott Sessions, when the Aztecs arrived in the Valley of Mexico in the early fourteenth century, "they found a Lake Culture where many towns and city-states were constantly trading, fighting and negotiating with one another."[1] All these groups sprang from a culture that traced back almost five hundred years. The Toltecs, a warlike society that thrived from 900 CE to 1200 CE, produced great artists and political leaders. They expanded their territories through military victories. The Toltecs' capital city, Tula, had been only fifty miles from the swampy lake the Aztecs would make their own capital, and Toltec influence throughout the area had been significant. The Toltecs worshiped the myth of Quetzalcoatl, the famed feathered serpent god who had been banished in a battle with the god of the night sky. Until Quetzalcoatl returned, the Toltecs believed they had to make blood sacrifices to the god of the night sky so that the sun would rise each day.

The Aztecs adopted the myth of Quetzalcoatl because it fit their blood-

Quetzalcoatl

Statues of fierce Toltec warriors more than one thousand years old stand in Tula, Mexico. The Aztecs took their sense of royal blood from the Toltecs, who had established themselves near the Valley of Mexico five hundred years earlier.

oriented culture. In time, Quetzalcoatl took a place alongside other Aztec gods such as Huitzilopochtli (the god of war) and Tlaloc (the god of rain and harvest) as symbols for numerous Aztec ceremonies. They supported the Toltec idea of human sacrifice in order to appease their gods. The Aztecs combined their worship of the sun with their need for bloodletting in order to justify the use of human sacrifice in all their rituals.

The Toltec-Aztec connection was cemented in the last half of the fourteenth century. The Aztecs, still not completely independent, offered one of their young men in marriage to a royal princess of nearby Culhuacan, which was the seat of what was left of Toltec society. The offer was accepted, the marriage took place, and in time a son was born. His name was Acamapichtli, and in 1375, he became the first king of an independent Aztec state.

A Hint of What
Was to Come

In the early 1300s, years before they had come upon the swampy lake that would be their permanent home, the Aztecs were living on the fringes of Culhuacan in the Valley of Mexico. The Culhua were among the elite societies in the Valley. They had hired the Aztecs as mercenaries after the Aztecs had attacked one of the Culhua's rivals and offered a bagful of cut-off ears from the defeated victims. The Culhua were impressed with the Aztecs' ferociousness and allowed them to settle on their lands.

Xipe

Since the Culhua claimed the Toltecs as ancestors, the Aztecs sought to affiliate themselves with the Toltecs, too. While we don't know where this story originated, what happened next may be part myth and part truth. The Aztecs offered one of their young men in marriage to a daughter of the Culhua king. In this way they could claim Toltec connection. The king agreed to the marriage and sent his daughter, along with gold and jewels, to the Aztec camp for the ceremony.

For the Aztecs, the girl's arrival represented a rare chance to celebrate the feast of Xipe Toltec. Xipe was the Aztec god of spring and new vegetation, as well as the patron of those who worked with gold. Celebrating him would require a special sacrifice. The arrival of the princess with her gold in preparation for marriage and eventual birth of a child was a sign the Aztecs could not ignore. She symbolized Xipe. Their gods had spoken.

They took the princess, performed a ritual sacrifice on her, then removed her skin.

Later, when the king arrived at the Xipe Toltec feast, he was greeted by an Aztec priest wearing his daughter's skin. Horrified, he banished the Aztecs from Culhuacan.

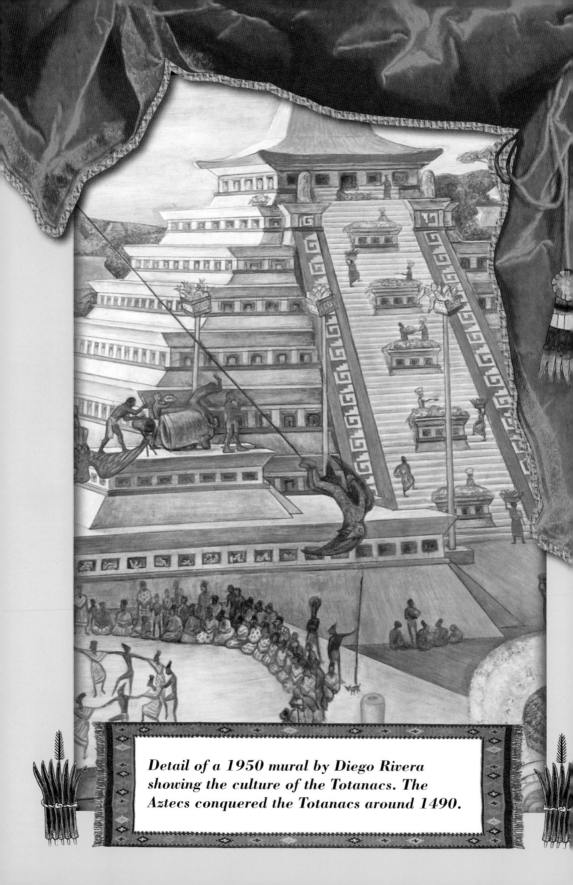

Detail of a 1950 mural by Diego Rivera showing the culture of the Totanacs. The Aztecs conquered the Totanacs around 1490.

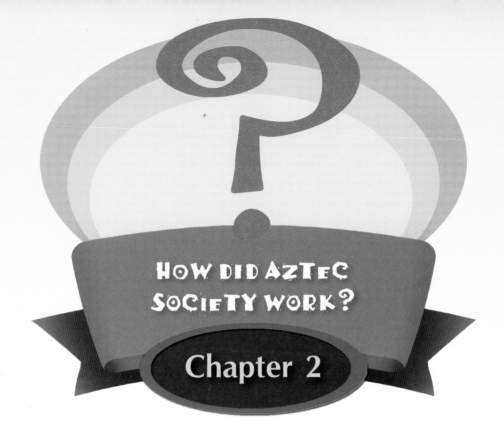

How did Aztec Society Work?

Chapter 2

When the Aztecs came upon that swampy island in 1325, they were little more than a wandering band without established leaders. True, they were fierce fighters, and they carried their imposing gods with them. Existing societies in the Valley of Mexico didn't want them around.

Once the Aztecs had a home, they dug canals and erected dikes and began to build a city that would rise above the swamp. They called their city Tenochtitlán, and gradually, other communities in the Valley of Mexico began to trade with them. The Aztecs acquired materials to build their city by trading "for swamp delicacies such as fish, frogs, ducks and algae,"[1] according to anthropologist Michael Smith. Still, they didn't feel strong enough to resist the most powerful states in the Valley of Mexico, so they worked as mercenaries while slowly building their own power.

By 1375, the Aztecs had their first *tlatoani*—the son of a princess from nearby Culhuacan. Now the Aztec state was equal to its neighbors. Even so, it continued to fight under the banner of its most powerful neighbor—the Tepanecs—for another fifty years. People began to stream into Tenochtitlán to live, and as the city grew, so did the Aztec reputation.

By 1427, the Aztecs were so powerful, they no longer had to act as mercenaries. In that year they elected Itzcóatl the new *tlatoani*. (Even though the *tlatoani* was a king, he was elected; rule was not inherited.) In one of his first acts, Itzcóatl led the Aztecs to victory over the Tepanecs, and finally the Aztecs paid tribute to no one. It was the beginning of the Aztec Empire, and there was no doubt the king was in charge.

Statue of Itzcóatl in the Garden of Triple Alliance

In the king's government, his number one assistant and chief adviser was the *cihuacoatl*, or prime minister, who was usually the high priest. Below the *cihuacoatl* came four military commanders called *tetecubtin*; each was responsible for a portion of the capital city. Under the military was the "supreme council" of about one hundred people who ran things day to day. Each member of the supreme council would have ties to individual neighborhoods (called *calpolli*) so that citizens could know what was going on. In this way the king communicated with everyone.

From the time of Itzcóatl, the Aztec Empire began to grow. Trade with other societies and states developed, and Aztec merchants began to travel outside the empire, sometimes for months and months. They would return with exotic goods—strange feathers, unusual jewels or metals—and exciting stories of new lands and new peoples. The traveling Aztec merchants also became a

spy network for the king, providing information on military strength and attitudes of the people toward their leaders in lands the Aztec kings might want to conquer. Merchants were treated well in Aztec society. They were like explorers or adventurers who could bring back riches while planting Aztec society in more and more places.

At the bottom of the social scale were slaves, and many Aztec nobles had them. Some were tribute from the states the Aztecs had conquered. Instead of offering them for sacrifice, some nobles kept the slaves to work at their homes and palaces. But an Aztec could also be a slave. If a person couldn't pay a debt, he could sell himself into slavery to the person he owed. Also, if a person committed a serious crime, such as robbery, he could be sentenced to become a slave to the person he had robbed.

However, an Aztec could never be born into slavery, and once someone had a slave, he or she was responsible for that slave's welfare.

Images from the **Florentine Codex,** *a book illustrated for the Spanish by Aztec artists, show an Aztec marketplace. Animal skins, jewelry, feathers, headdresses, maguey, and cotton cloth were among the most frequently traded objects.*

An Aztec slave market; the slave wears a wooden collar. Slavery was an important part of the Aztec Empire, providing labor and wealth to owners.

Slaves could marry, have children, and even own property, and a slave could not be transferred to another owner without the slave's consent.

Two other things were unusual about slavery in the Aztec Empire. First, since slaves were able to own property, they could buy their way to freedom, so slavery was never a life sentence. Second, slaves were allowed to own slaves, too.

From the king at the top to the slave's slave at the bottom, Aztec society was running smoothly.

An Aztec turquoise and gold necklace

Montezuma's Rules

When Itzcóatl died in 1440, his nephew, Montezuma, was elected to succeed him. Montezuma, who is also known as Motecuhzoma, Moctezuma, and Moteuczoma, would reign for twenty-nine years. Under his leadership, Aztec power would grow and expand until it stretched beyond the Valley of Mexico to what we now know as the Gulf of Mexico. Montezuma saw himself as something greater than a mere mortal, not fully divine but a cut or two above the average citizen. By this time Aztec society had developed two distinct classes: the nobles and the commoners. Montezuma decided that each of these groups needed special rules for daily living, and he issued a legal code that spelled out the rights each would have. Here are a few of the rules:

- Only the king and the prime minister . . . may wear sandals within the palace . . .
- The commoners will not be allowed to wear cotton clothing, under pain of death, but can use only garments of maguey fiber [rough cloth made from the maguey cactus plant] . . .
- Only the great noblemen and valiant warriors are given license to build a house with a second story; for disobeying this law a person receives the death penalty . . .
- Only the great lords are to wear labrets [lip plugs], ear plugs, and nose plugs of gold and precious stones . . .[2]

Montezuma, however, was not blind to people improving themselves. He created a new title, *quauhpilli* (literally: eagle lord), for commoners who distinguished themselves in battle. He allowed these *quauhpilli* to rise to positions of influence while remaining commoners.

Montezuma I

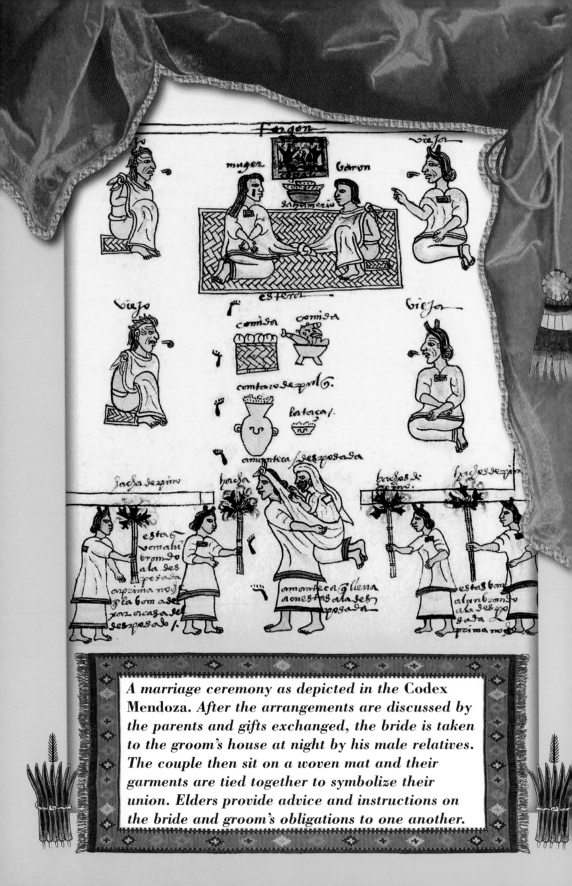

A marriage ceremony as depicted in the Codex Mendoza. After the arrangements are discussed by the parents and gifts exchanged, the bride is taken to the groom's house at night by his male relatives. The couple then sit on a woven mat and their garments are tied together to symbolize their union. Elders provide advice and instructions on the bride and groom's obligations to one another.

WHAT WAS AN AZTEC FAMILY LIKE?

Chapter 3

As the sun peeked over the horizon each morning, the Aztec family awoke to trumpets and shell horns blowing from the nearby temple. In their mostly stone houses, the entire family slept in a single room on rough mats raised off the dirt floor. After bathing and dressing (the men in loincloths, the women in long skirts and embroidered blouses), it was off to work for the men while the women swept their houses, ground corn for tortillas, and spun and wove cotton and maguey cloth. Cotton fabric was made exclusively for nobles and was a finer texture than maguey. By law, no commoners could wear cotton.

Most commoners lived in neighborhoods (called *calpolli*), and the neighborhood was overseen by nobles who lived in nearby compounds and palaces. Often, several commoner generations lived under the same roof or in a cluster of homes opening to a common patio, and several of these home clusters would make up a *calpolli*. Commoners saw their *calpolli* as the center of their lives. Nobles owned all the land and were in charge of everything: the government, army, and commerce. Commoners served them and lived on the nobles' land, usually paying an annual tribute. But nobles also felt obligations to their own families. Franciscan Friar Bernardino de Sahagún, who lived with the Aztecs in

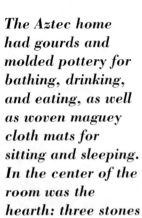

The Aztec home had gourds and molded pottery for bathing, drinking, and eating, as well as woven maguey cloth mats for sitting and sleeping. In the center of the room was the hearth: three stones supporting a clay disk on which tortillas were cooked.

1529 and from whom much of our information comes, recorded what a noble said to his son: "Listen . . . ye were born by the grace of our lords . . . ye were born not among the herbs, in the woods. And what are ye to do? . . . Take care of the drum, the gourd rattle . . . pay attention to artisanship, the art of feather working, the knowledge of things."[1]

The birth of a child was very important in Aztec life. The birthing ceremony was overseen by a midwife, who gave the baby its first bath, decided what its name would be, and informed the child how it was expected to conduct its life. Then the family summoned a soothsayer who consulted the stars, questioned the family, and examined pictographs to determine the signs that would govern the child's life. For boys, symbols included tools used by the boy's father in his work, while for girls, the symbols were a distaff with its spindle, basket, and broom. Thus, within two weeks of his or her birth, the blueprint of a child's life was laid out.

Naming the child Ten Rabbit

Most weddings in the Aztec world were arranged through matchmakers. Men were often in their late teens or early twenties, but women tended to be much younger. Before the marriage could go forward, the priests were consulted to see if the signs were favorable, and the groom's teachers were asked to comment. Then the elderly relatives of bride and groom sat them down and spoke about treating each other with respect and leading a virtuous life. After this, the wedding celebrations could begin.

Death in the Aztec world was marked by ritual. "Some people were buried in the fields; others in the courtyards of their own homes," wrote Friar Diego Durán, who studied Aztec society extensively in the sixteenth century. "Others were cremated and their ashes buried in the temples." All were dressed in their favorite capes, surrounded by special jewelry and stones. "No . . . possessions were left behind."[2]

Whether buried or cremated, the funeral activities lasted for up to ten days, with mourners coming from close and far away. There were drinking and eating and constant sorrowful chanting throughout the mourning period. To the Aztecs, the gods were watching and waiting for the soul of the deceased.

When someone got sick, the Aztecs would point to one of three causes, which would determine the cure. (1) If the illness was thought to be the result of a particular god's displeasure (in all, the Aztecs had more than 200 gods), confession to a priest or making religious offerings was needed. (2) If a *tlacatecolotl*, or evil sorcerer, had cast a spell,

The Aztecs believed in natural herbal plant remedies to help cure illnesses. In 1570, Spanish physician Francisco Hernández compiled a book describing Aztec medicinal plants. The book was destroyed by fire in 1671.

then rubbing and waving precious stones and drinking strange things such as skunk blood was needed to remove the spell. (3) If the illness was from natural causes, then it should be treated by a doctor. Herbs were the main ingredients in Aztec medicine. They grew well in the Valley of Mexico, and the doctors—both men and women—were skillful and experienced.

What made a good doctor? Here are a few requirements, as listed by Friar Bernardino de Sahagún:

- he is a wise man
- he has worked with herbs, stones, trees and roots
- he examines, he experiments
- he massages aches and sets broken bones
- he bleeds his patients
- he cuts and he sews the wound[3]

Except for bleeding the patient, most doctors today would fit this description.

The Formal Marriage Ceremony

Weddings were family affairs in the Aztec world, with both bride and groom families involved from the beginning. Once the matchmakers had completed their work, the two families took over. At midday on a day chosen because of its favorable signs, an elaborate feast at the bride's house would start things off. The bride's mother and other female relatives would have spent weeks preparing the food, and each guest was offered not only food but flowers, tobacco and drink. At sunset, the bride's female family members gave her a special bath. They cleansed her with soap, added perfume, decorated her with red feathers, and sprinkled yellow paint on her face.

Elders from the groom's family spoke to her: "Forever now leave childishness, girlishness; no longer art thou to be like a child," they lectured. "Respect your husband to be, remember your domestic responsibilities, take care of the sweeping, the laying of the fire . . ."[4]

Then, singing and dancing along the way, the groom's relatives carried the bride to the groom's house, where he was waiting in a private room. She was placed on a large woven reed mat opposite the groom while a fire burned behind them. The families entered the room and the groom's mother offered a new *huipilli* (female blouse) to the bride. The bride's mother returned the favor by tying a new cape on the groom and placing a new loincloth in front of him.

Up stepped the matchmakers, who tied a corner of the groom's new cape to the new *huipilli*, symbolically "tying the marriage knot." After feeding the couple a ritual meal, the matchmakers led them to a private bedchamber, where the bride and groom had to remain for four days.

On the fifth day, they came out of the room, and the wedding feast began. There was dancing, gifts were exchanged, and there were speeches about their responsibilities to one another and how they should conduct their lives.

At the end of the wedding feast, the families, in the words of anthropologist Michael Smith, returned home "content . . . feeling good in their hearts."[5]

Ancient ceremonial area of Templo Mayor, where the high priest performed sacrifices. Templo Mayor was the most important temple in the Aztec world.

WHAT ABOUT FOOD, FEASTING, AND FUN?

Chapter 4

Few expected a great city to arise when the Aztecs first saw Lake Texcoco in 1325. But a century and a half later—by 1475—Tenochtitlán had become one of the largest cities in the world, with more than two hundred thousand people. It was the heart of the Aztec Empire, and the seat of their most famous temple, the Templo Mayor.

An Aztec chili

The Aztecs used the rich, wet soil to build *chinampas,* or rectangular ground plots, by scooping out mud and piling it until it rose above the swamp surface. Then they spread the soil into earthen platforms—some 300 feet long—on which they could build and plant. In this nutrient-rich mud, the Aztecs planted their most important crop: maize (corn). This grain was the basis for tortillas, tamales, and other favorite Aztec foods, and no household was without a large supply of cornmeal. Other crops grown on the chinampas included beans, which were served at every meal; tomatoes; squash; avocados; and different types of chili peppers.

Much of what was grown on the *chinampas* would also be for sale in various village markets around the empire. The

Chinampas, or "mud islands," were built for growing fruits and vegetables in the Aztec Empire. The mud was dug from the bottom of the lake and built up until it created an island above the level of the water.

largest of these was the great market at Tlatelolco, a city very close to Tenochtitlán. When Hernán Cortés, leader of the Spanish conquistadores, saw Tlatelolco, he wrote: "There are daily more than sixty thousand folk buying and selling . . . all kinds of vegetables . . . many different sorts of fruits . . . all kinds of cotton thread . . . a great deal of chinaware . . . maize . . . pastries made from game and fish pies . . ."[1]

The Aztecs had another important crop: cacao beans, used to make chocolate, which was an Aztec delicacy. The beans were also used as currency because the Aztecs didn't have money (bills and coins) like we have. They exchanged cacao beans when they made small purchases (such as a tamale or chopped firewood), and each family kept a supply of beans just as families today keep money in a checking account to buy groceries and pay bills.

For more expensive purchases, the Aztecs used *quachtli* or cotton capes, and they traded them as they would trade cacao beans. Since cotton cloth could be worn only by nobles,

quachtli

its value was high, and many cacao beans were needed to pay for a single cape. One standard-size *quachtli* might cost 65 to 80 cacao beans.

The Aztecs celebrated many festivals during the year, including eighteen that some scholars believe involved public sacrifice. They base their beliefs on surviving documents and pictographs from the Aztec culture. However, not everyone agrees on how to interpret these artifacts, and some have made the case there was not much sacrifice in the Aztec world. There's no doubt, however, that the Aztecs had a lot of festivals. They celebrated everything from paying debts to receiving rain from the rain god. They developed their own calendar, too, so they knew when each festival would happen. Since many festivals had religious themes, the local temple would be involved. In Tenochtitlán, the religious center was the Templo Mayor. It towered 197 feet over the city, with many steps leading to the top. Further shrines to Huitzilo-pochtli, the god of war, and Tlaloc, the rain god, rose from the top,

In the Tenochtitlán market, Aztec families could buy goods of all kinds, including animals and birds. There were numerous markets throughout the Aztec Empire.

Reenactors play an ancient Aztec ballgame in which players had to put a ball through a small hole in a stone ring above their heads. They could not touch the ball with their hands.

and it was there, at the base of the shrines, that the high priests performed their most important sacrifices.

A highlight of many festivals was the ballgame, which can be traced to the Olmecs more than three thousand years ago. Men, women, children, and even royalty played it, sometimes betting their homes, wives, children, or slaves on the result.

The ballgame was played on an I-shaped court 100 to 200 feet long, with a center line and spectators on each side. Two stone rings three feet in diameter were set into the wall, and the object was to get a nine-pound rubber ball through one of the hoops without using the hands. The ball could be hit with the elbows, knees, hips, and head only. The ball was not supposed to touch the ground, and players threw themselves all over the court to keep the ball in play. When the ballgame was over, many were bleeding and battered.

And the spectators loved it!

In the Aztec world it was important to mark religious dates, to predict lucky and unlucky days, and to pay attention to the passing of the years. The Aztecs used three separate calendars: a 260-day calendar for predicting the future, a 365-day calendar for keeping track of public ceremonies, and a 52-year calendar for the end and renewal of their civilization (see Introduction: The New Fire Ceremony).

In the 260-day calendar, they had 20 separate days, calling them (as translated) *crocodile, wind, house*, and other nouns. Then they applied numbers 1 through 13 to each named day, with the numbers starting over after 13. There would be two separate columns:

named days
crocodile
wind
house . . .

numbered days
1, 8
2, 9
3, 10 . . .

The 21st named day would be *crocodile* again and be numbered day 8. Then, instead of predicting a successful harvest on "August 10," the calendar would show it happening on *3 house* or *8 crocodile*. Twenty named days times thirteen numbered days equals 260, and once that number was reached, the cycle started over again.

The 365-day calendar followed the 20-name-day cycle, but to keep track of the seasons, the Aztecs used 18 months (not 12 as we do) and then added 5 additional days at the end. Each month had 20 days, divided into four weeks of five days each. This gave them a yearlong calendar just like ours, and they could plan for festivals and ceremonies.

The 52-year calendar totaled 18,980 days (52 years of 365 days each). The Aztecs used four revolving names: *calli, tochtli, acatl, tecpatl* (meaning: house, rabbit, reed, flint knife), and combined them with revolving numbers 1 through 13 (just as with the 260-day calendar). In this way, each year had its own name and number: *1 calli, 3 acatl, 6 tochtli*, and so forth. Using this system, the Aztecs could pinpoint any years in their 52-year cycle.

Aztec parents, in traditional loincloths and capes, walk their children to school.

WHAT WAS SCHOOL LIKE?

Chapter 5

Family life was very important to the Aztecs. Children were cherished, and the birth of a child was cause for great celebration. Parents and grandparents were admired and respected. Adults, including the emperor, took serious responsibility for guiding young people along proper paths of self-discipline and humility. Aztec poets portrayed what that training would create:

> The mature man:
> a heart as firm as stone,
> a wise countenance,
> the owner of a face, a heart,
> capable of understanding.[1]

For Aztec society, schooling and learning were crucial. In fact, Montezuma I (who was king from 1440 to 1458) decreed that every young person had to go to school. He also required that schools be built in every *calpolli* in the empire.

However, up to age fifteen, education was left to parents. They had the responsibility to guide boys and girls along paths of self-reliance

Male children (left) learn to work hard, to hunt, and to fish, while female children learn how to keep a home, to cook, and to weave.

and humility. Boys were to develop both physically and mentally into spartan-like sturdiness. Girls were to develop a sense about the home and learn skills such as weaving and spinning. When the children reached fifteen, they would be ready for the next step: attending school outside the home.

There were two types of schools: one for nobles and one for commoners. The sons of noble families went to the *calmecac,* a school tied to a major temple. They were trained to become future leaders of the empire, and they were exposed to harsh training, laboring in the fields, gathering firewood at all hours, and being punished for breaking the smallest of rules. Priests and other highly respected adults, including top military and governmental officials, guided them. The *calmecacs* continued to stress the spartan-like lifestyle parents had developed in their children. Encouraged were self-control, discipline, and obedience.

Commoners attended *telpochcalli* (literally, "youth houses"). These were in every town or *calpolli.* Boys and girls were separated, and the boys were trained to become good soldiers. Girls were taught weaving,

spinning, and sewing, and how to prepare a proper home. Both boys and girls lived at their *telpochcalli,* and they had few luxuries. They rose at dawn, and learned or worked throughout the day, often doing the most difficult tasks their elders could devise. As with the sons of nobles in the *calmecacs,* life in the *telpochcalli* for the sons and daughters of commoners was spartan, with early rising, hard work, and few comforts.

There were also schools that trained young people to sing sacred songs and perform the ritual dances of the Aztec culture. Known as *cuicacalli,* these were associated with temples and run by priests. Instruction would begin an hour before sunset and continue well into the night. The songs covered the history and traditions of the Aztec people, touching on myths—such as their ancestors' departure from Aztlán—as well as actual events, such as Aztec army victories. Praise for

Children learned to play the rattle, the whistle, the trumpet, the flute, the copper bells, and drums. They would play music and dance with hundreds of other people in sacred rituals.

cipactli crocodile	ehecatl wind	calli house	cuetzpalin lizard	coatl snake
miquiztli death	mazatl deer	tochtli rabbit	atl water	itzcuintli dog
ozomahtli monkey	malinalli grass	acatl reed	ocelotl jaguar	cuauhtli eagle
cozcacuauhtli vulture	ollin motion	tecpatl flint	quiahuitl rain	xochitl flower

The Aztecs used pictographs to tell stories of their civilization and to designate days, months, and years on their calendars.

the gods, their relationship to the culture, and the responsibilities everyone had for carrying out the gods' wishes were important parts of the songs and dances. For young people, the experience gave them a sense of unity. According to religious historians Carrasco and Sessions, it made them proud to be Aztecs.[2]

Much of the teaching was oral: Stories and lessons were told, not written. But Aztecs also used pictographs (sometimes carved in stone, sometimes painted on bark) to embellish their stories and lessons. These pictographs contained glyphs—signs that stood for a word, sound, or idea, and the Aztec culture had several hundred well-recognized glyphs. For example, a dot meant "one," a flag meant "20," a feather meant "400." A pictograph showing a flag followed by the outline of a warrior dragging a prisoner meant that 20 prisoners had been taken in a particular Aztec victory. The pictographs often showed important people, places, or events, but the teacher (usually a priest or noble) used them as story guidelines, not as the complete story. The teacher would add his own personal knowledge and fill in the story, interpreting the glyphs and providing a more complete picture.

Learning Through
Riddles and Proverbs

The Aztecs used riddles and proverbs to strengthen the students' sense of place in the world. Riddles were expressed as questions, but note how the answers provide a picture:

Q: What is a little blue-green jar filled with popcorn . . . ?
A: . . . the sky
Q: What is a mountainside that has a spring of water in it?
A: Our nose
Q: What is that which is a small mirror in a house made of fir branches?
A: Our eye
Q: What is it that goes along the foothills of the mountain, patting our tortillas with its hands?
A: A butterfly!
Q: What is that which we enter in three places and leave by only one?
A: Our shirt.[3]

Aztec butterfly symbol

Proverbs were used to educate and inspire. They provided a picture through words, offering images and lessons:

- *Because of him my face becomes wide*—often used to describe a well-brought up or well-taught child
- *Already at the edge of the fire; Already at the stairway*—someone about to be put to death or whose time it was to be put to death
- *In the Clouds; In the Mist*—someone highly esteemed, someone very great, someone never before seen or never known. When the Spaniards first came in 1519 (and destroyed the Aztec Empire two years later), they were said to have come from the clouds and the mist.
- *I heed no mother, I heed no father*—someone who has been disciplined many times but never seems to learn.[4]

Note the importance of discipline, respect for elders, and attention paid to how a young person behaves. When we say, "Children should be seen but not heard," or "Spare the rod and spoil the child," we are offering our own proverbs.

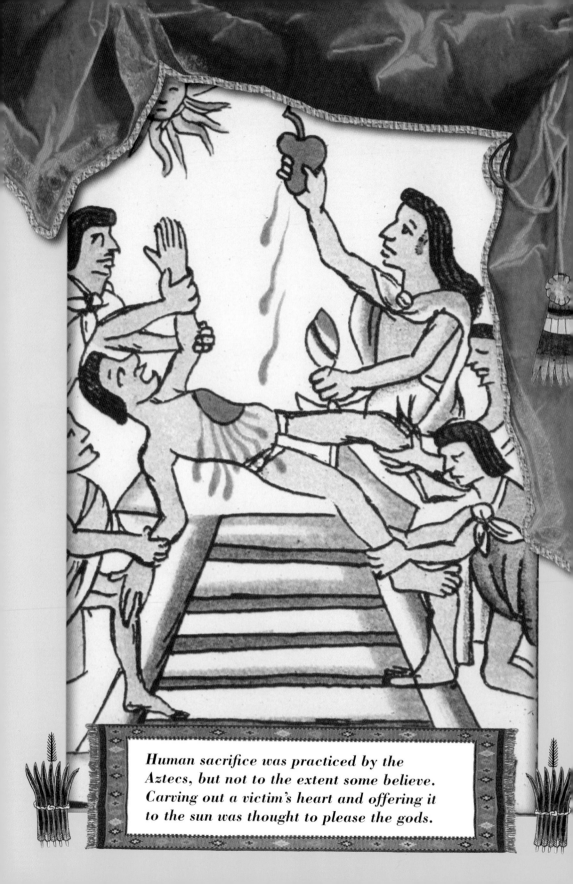

Human sacrifice was practiced by the Aztecs, but not to the extent some believe. Carving out a victim's heart and offering it to the sun was thought to please the gods.

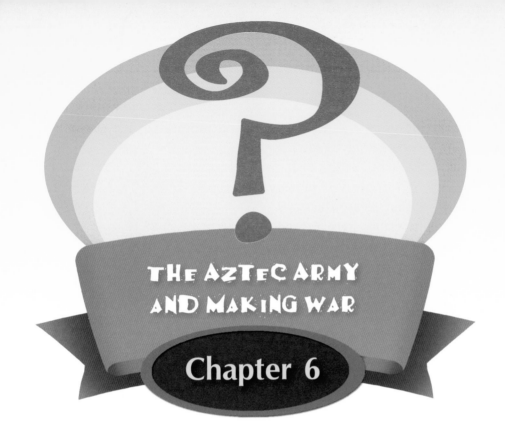

THE AZTEC ARMY AND MAKING WAR

Chapter 6

For the Aztecs, waging war was essential. War not only built the empire but also pleased the Aztec gods. War gave the Aztecs a chance to take prisoners, whom they could use for human sacrifice. Historians are not sure how often the Aztecs practiced human sacrifice, but many scholars believe they did so from time to time, especially to celebrate important events. They would sacrifice victims to their gods, especially to their god of war, Huitzilopochtli, whose temple sat atop the huge Templo Mayor in Tenochtitlán. They believed Huitzilopochtli also represented the sun, and the sun needed human blood from sacrifice to maintain domination over the moon and stars. Otherwise, total darkness would come.

The Aztecs did not put one of their own people in charge after winning a war; they allowed the conquered *tlatoani* to remain. They also did not occupy the conquered territory. What they wanted was tribute, and the conquered state would agree to pay it, usually every year. Tribute included cotton capes, warrior costumes and shields, tropical feathers (which were considered a luxury), cacao beans, maize, gold dust, and precious stones. In this way the wealth of the Aztec Empire would grow.

Warrior shield made from maguey fabric and feathers

Warriors were trained to wound and capture an enemy, not kill him. A dead enemy was of little value, because he could not be offered in sacrifice. A live prisoner was precious, because his sacrifice would please the gods.

Aztec warriors were ranked on how many prisoners they captured. A one-captive warrior would be rewarded with a *manta*, or cloak, decorated with flowers. A two-captive warrior was allowed to wear specially decorated sandals, a cone-shaped cap, and a feathered warrior suit. A four-captive warrior wore a jaguar skin over his body into battle, and he was given a high military rank. Jaguars were ferocious hunters, and the Aztecs adopted them as symbols for their bravest warriors. Such warriors would be knighted by the king: "The hair on the top of his head was parted in two [by the king], and red cord wrapped around it; in the same cord was attached an ornament of green, blue and red feathers . . . and a red tassel," wrote Friar Diego Durán.[1]

When going into battle, the Aztec warrior wore an *ichcahuipilli,* a suit of heavy, salt-saturated quilt about two fingers thick. Over this he wore a feathered tunic or jumpsuit of heavy cloth. Warriors carried round shields made of wood and leather, and swords and clubs fitted with sharp, embedded obsidian glass. They also used bows and arrows, slings, wooden darts, and lances. But should a warrior be killed in battle, it was not a time of sorrow. The Aztecs considered death in combat a great sacrifice to the gods, something to be honored. They also held a special ceremony, "gladiatorial sacrifice," when they captured an especially ferocious enemy. The prisoner would be tied by the leg to a large round stone and provided

Reconstruction of an ichcahuipilli and helmet

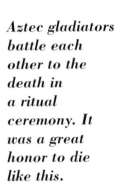

Aztec gladiators battle each other to the death in a ritual ceremony. It was a great honor to die like this.

The macuahuitl (weapon) would have been fitted with glass.

with harmless, though symbolic, weapons. An Aztec warrior, using regular weapons, would fight him and kill him. The prisoner's body would then be offered for sacrifice, and that would please the gods.

Commoners made up the bulk of the Aztec army. Nobles were usually the ranking officers, but commoners could gain prestige and higher rank by capturing enemy soldiers. Emperor Montezuma I even created a special title, *quauhpilli,* for the bravest warriors, and these fighters enjoyed some of the same privileges as the nobles. They were known as "nobles by achievement" rather than nobles by birth, and they were held in high esteem.

As their society grew stronger in the early fifteenth century, the Aztecs began to think about dominating neighbors outside as well as inside the Valley of Mexico. Emperor Itzcóatl, who had begun expanding the Aztec homeland with small victories, realized he needed a stronger and larger army to wage war outside the Valley of Mexico. In 1428, he formed the Triple Alliance with

Warrior ranks in the Aztec army. Those wearing eagle or jaguar headdresses were considered the bravest and most accomplished.

the states of Texcoco on the east and Tlacopan to the north. They combined their forces, and with each victory, they split up the tribute: two-fifths to Tenochtitlán, two-fifths to Texcoco, one-fifth to Tlacopan. The arrangement worked so well that by the time the Spanish arrived in 1519, the Triple Alliance was receiving tribute from 38 conquered states and controlled most of central Mexico from the Pacific Ocean to the Gulf of Mexico.

Young boys in warrior training

Flower Wars

In about 1450, during the reign of Montezuma I, Tlacaelel, Montezuma's brother, made arrangements with several states on or near the borders to fight battles that would produce sacrifice victims. The goal was not to conquer their neighbors, but to practice warfare and acquire prisoners to be sacrificed to their gods.

Several of the neighboring states shared a common language—Nahuatl—with the Aztecs, as well as a common culture, so they had similar attitudes toward sacrifice and the gods. Fighting to conquer one another made little sense. Instead, Tlacaelel made agreements with the leaders of Tlaxcala, Cholula, Huexotzinco, and Tiliuhquitepec, all neighboring states, to wage "ritual" wars where the sole object was to take prisoners. The states would agree ahead of time when the battles would begin, how many would be involved, and where they would take place. That doesn't mean the wars weren't fought ferociously or that some warriors weren't killed, but in the end there would be no victor, no tribute given, and no territory taken.

Jaguar warrior

The Aztecs called this type of warfare *xochiyaoyotl*, literally "flower wars" or "practice wars." In addition to acquiring sacrifice victims, some believe the Aztecs also had political motives. Since their empire was larger than the other states, they could show off their military strength and emphasize how powerful they were. Who, then, would want to challenge them in all-out combat?

Warriors of the Triple Alliance

In modern Mexico City stands a sculpture of the eagle on a cactus, clutching a snake in its claws—the sign that told the Aztecs they had found their home in the Valley of Mexico. The statues to the right commemorate the founding of Tenochtitlán (Mexico City).

HOW DID THEY CREATE ART AND BEAUTY?

Chapter 7

The Aztecs had a deep appreciation for art and beauty. In particular, they loved language and the way words could be spoken. They used speechmaking to showcase skills as orators and to provide the story of their culture. Speakers offered elaborate tales of historical events, tied in with legends of ancestors and their gods (including the mythical departure from Aztlán, the wanderings of many centuries, and the appearance of the sign—an eagle perched on a cactus with a rattlesnake in its claws—promised by Huitzilopochtli). These tales were what we call "oral history" because no one wrote them down, but they would be repeated to the next generation, who would then hand them down to the next generation and so forth. In this way the tales were connected through the centuries.

Often, the oratory took the form of poetry (which was highly respected by the Aztecs). The orator might talk of a suffering heart that looks for beauty (to the Aztecs, the heart was the crucial connection between human beings and the sun, which provides life on earth. During sacrifice, the victim's heart was offered to the sun in an effort to please the god of the sun). This Aztec poem shows how beauty—in the form of flowers and song—eases the suffering of the heart:

> Eagerly does my heart yearn for flowers;
> I suffer with songs, yet I create them on earth . . .
> I crave flowers that will not perish in my hands!
> Where might I find lovely flowers, lovely songs?
> Such as I seek, spring does not produce on earth . . .[1]

Montezuma II's headdress

The Aztecs saw all forms of art as divine. Through art, a person could receive communication from the gods. Art showed how beauty could be transmitted by the gods, and it celebrated the power and the beauty of the gods so that life on earth would benefit. But art to the Aztecs was more than spoken or written. Artists also made things by hand. The most important artisans were the feather makers. A feathered headdress, for example, was one of the most sought-after items. Feathers also adorned fans and capes, warrior outfits, and shields. Feather workers were commoners whose skills lay in arranging the feathers and mixing the colors. They used plumage from numerous tropical birds, including the quetzal, the macaw, and the toucan. It was said that when Emperor Montezuma II met the Spanish for the first time in 1519, he wore a headdress that contained the feathers of more than 250 tropical birds.

Quetzal

Statue of Coatlicue

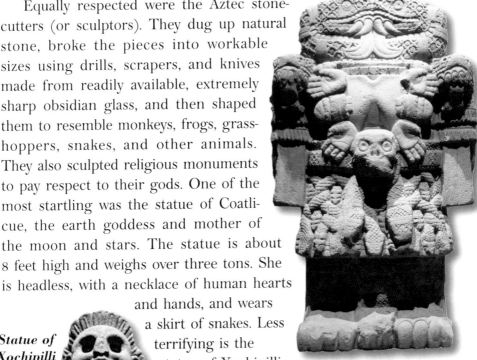

Equally respected were the Aztec stone-cutters (or sculptors). They dug up natural stone, broke the pieces into workable sizes using drills, scrapers, and knives made from readily available, extremely sharp obsidian glass, and then shaped them to resemble monkeys, frogs, grass-hoppers, snakes, and other animals. They also sculpted religious monuments to pay respect to their gods. One of the most startling was the statue of Coatli-cue, the earth goddess and mother of the moon and stars. The statue is about 8 feet high and weighs over three tons. She is headless, with a necklace of human hearts and hands, and wears a skirt of snakes. Less

Statue of Xochipilli

terrifying is the statue of Xochipilli, the god of love and summertime, who is seated and quietly thinking. To the Aztecs, he was the Prince of Flowers.

Another form of art was the sculpting of precious gems such as turquoise and jade. Gems might be fixed to capes of nobles and royalty, others could be embedded in the handles of knives or in decorative pottery. Frequently, tiles of turquoise contained shells or dark obsidian glass, which gave color contrast. Nobles wore jade lip plugs as status symbols. Commoners, of course, were not allowed to wear lip plugs or to possess anything embedded with precious stones.

Aztec metal-workers heated raw copper and gold to form it into jewelry, trinkets, and ornaments for capes and weapons.

The Aztecs formed molds to shape molten silver and gold into necklaces, bracelets, or earrings. Goldworking, considered a "luxury craft in the Valley of Mexico,"[2] sometimes included jade beads or other embedded precious stones.

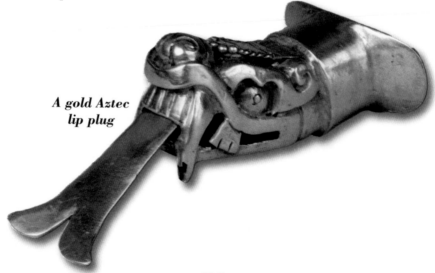

A gold Aztec lip plug

The Aztec Calendar Stone

Perhaps the most famous piece of Aztec stone sculpture ever discovered is the Calendar Stone. Aztec myth, legend, and history are laid out on the face of this single huge rock. The stone was carved during the fifteenth century and finished in 1479, when the Aztec Empire was all-powerful. It stands about thirteen feet high, weighs about 24 tons, and shows how the Aztecs divided their year into 18 months of 20 days each plus five days at the end (see "How the Aztecs Told Time," page 33). Aztec priests used the stone to highlight upcoming festivals and ceremonies, and by reading the stone, they could pinpoint the hour of the day and track the sun's progress through the sky.

The stone has an outer border showing two serpents, representing time and various Aztec gods. Rays shoot up to the border from the center of the stone, where there is carved the fierce face of the sun god. His tongue sticks out, representing the knife used in human sacrifice. On either side are sharp claws grasping a human heart. The meaning is clear: To appease this god, there must be human sacrifice.

Around the sun god are several concentric rings containing symbols and glyphs. For example, the second ring shows the days of the Aztec month as glyphs (such as snake, house, and wind). There are 20 glyph squares, with each portraying one of the 20 days in the Aztec month. Five dots show up inside the ring, and these represent the 5 leftover days in each year. The third ring shows a series of small squares, each filled with five balls, and the balls represent the Aztec week of five days, with the squares representing the weeks.

Most consider the Aztec Calendar Stone the finest piece of Aztec stonework ever found. It was discovered in 1790, long after the Spanish conquest of Mexico, and it rests in the National Museum of Anthropology in Mexico City.

Hernán Cortés and Montezuma II meeting at the outskirts of Tenochtitlán in 1519, where Montezuma would present Cortés with a gold necklace. This painting is based on contemporary sketches of the scene.

THE END OF AN EMPIRE

Epilogue

In 1519, when Hernán Cortés and about 500 Spanish soldiers landed on the gulf coast of Mexico, near what is now Vera Cruz, few would have believed that two years later the Aztec Empire would be in ruins. The Spanish had heard rumors of a rich and powerful kingdom, of gold and silver and precious stones in abundance.

They came at the height of the Aztec Empire's power. Montezuma II had led Aztec armies to 44 conquests since he came to power in 1502, and more than 370 city-states were paying annual tribute. The yearly amounts included 7,000 tons of corn, 4,000 tons of beans, and 2 million cotton capes for the more than one million people in the Valley of Mexico. Montezuma II had declared himself divine. Noblemen carried his litter when he traveled. Whoever appeared before him had to come barefoot with eyes downcast, and they did not turn their back when leaving his presence. His armies numbered in the thousands, and his soldiers offered unquestioned loyalty.

How could a ragged band of 500 Spaniards trudging through unfamiliar land possibly handle such a ferocious, well-disciplined army?

Good luck helped. In the years before the arrival of the Spaniards, unsettling omens had appeared to the Aztecs: fire burned down the temple of Huitzilopochtli, the god of war; lightning struck the temple of the god of fire; a comet appeared going west to east across the sky, trailing a fiery tail; the lakes around Tenochtitlán burst their banks and flooded many homes.

The Aztecs interpreted these disasters as signs of impending doom caused by the gods' displeasure. When the Spanish in their strange-looking armor, carrying strange weapons, came face to face with the Aztecs, the reaction was fear. The Spanish appeared to be messengers of the gods sent to destroy the empire. As Cortés neared Tenochtitlán, Montezuma kept sending elaborate gold gifts and beautiful feather work, urging him to go away. According to a Spanish priest who witnessed it, the Aztecs "laid before [the Spaniards] golden streamers, quetzal feather streamers, and golden necklaces . . . [the Spaniards] thirsted mightily for gold; they stuffed themselves with it, and starved and lusted for it like pigs."[1]

Pedro de Alvarado

Cortés quietly built an army from resentful city-states who had been paying tribute to the Aztecs. Soon he could field an army of thousands.

They marched on Tenochtitlán, and Montezuma came out to meet them. He climbed from his litter, Cortés jumped from his horse, and the two men embraced. A witness to the meeting added: "From one of his noblemen [Montezuma] took a splendid necklace of gold, inlaid with precious stones and placed it around Cortés's neck."[2] Montezuma invited the Spaniards into his city.

Soon, however, relations soured. Cortés, noting the fabulous riches in Tenochtitlán, wanted some for himself and his men, and he wanted to stop the Aztecs' use of human sacrifice. He took Montezuma prisoner.

In 1521, Tenochtitlán fell as Cortés laid seige to the city and the Aztec Empire.

Pedro de Alvarado, Cortés' assistant, heard about a planned human sacrifice ceremony to honor Huitzilopochtli. Alvarado gathered his troops, who attacked and massacred many of the participants. The Aztecs were enraged and fought back, sending the Spanish fleeing across the nearby mountains. Montezuma II died in the fighting, and a new *tlatoani* was elected.

Several months later, Cortés returned, this time with 700 Spanish soldiers and more than 70,000 non-Aztec troops. After fierce fighting, the Aztec army was pushed back into Tenochtitlán, and a siege began. The Spaniards cut off fresh water supplies and blocked shipments of food. In a few months, a plague of smallpox decimated the Aztecs. A Spanish priest recounted what he had been told by witnesses: "The illness was so dreadful that no one could talk or move. The sick were so utterly helpless that they could only lie on the beds like corpses."[3]

In the end, about 40 percent of the population of Tenochtitlán and the Valley of Mexico died from the smallpox plague. The Aztecs fought on, and on August 13, 1521, the Spanish captured Cuauhtémoc, the final Aztec *tlatoani.* The Aztec Empire was no more.

HOW TO MAKE A FEATHER HEADDRESS

The jeweled headdress that is thought to have belonged to Monte-zuma II has at least 450 long green feathers from the quetzal bird. You can make a headdress like his, but you can get away with using just a few dozen feathers—or construction paper—instead.

What You Will Need
Two paper plates
Scissors
String
Glue
Green construction paper or several dozen long green feathers
 (available at craft stores)
Red paint and paintbrush or markers
Small, fluffy feathers such as marabou (available at craft stores)

1   Fold a paper plate in half, with the top of the plate to the inside. Cut a circle from the center of the plate. Be sure to cut enough away for the arch to fit comfortably over your head.

2   Cut two pieces of string, long enough to reach from the top of your head and tie under your chin. Lay one piece of string along either crease in the plate. Place one end of the string even with the outside of the plate, and let the long side dangle down on the cut side of the crease. Tape the string in place.

3   Place the shafts of several dozen long green feathers inside the folded plate. Fan them out over the top arch. Glue them, and the string, in place.

    If you have a hard time finding long green feathers, you can use green construction paper to make this part of the headdress. Fold the paper in half lengthwise, then cut slits down from the open edge of the paper toward the middle. Do not cut the paper all the way to the fold; you will glue that part of the paper inside the plate. To make the paper look more like feathers, cut the ends of the little strips into points.

4   From the other paper plate, cut a piece from the edge that is about two inches wide and two inches long. Glue it to the middle front of the headdress, as shown in the picture. Let the glue dry.

5   Once the glue is dry, you can decorate the headdress. Use red paint or markers to color the arch of the plate, but leave the edge of the plate white. After the paint dries, glue smaller blue and green feathers in an arch to match Montezuma's headdress.

6   After everything is dry, tie your headdress on.

1200–400 BCE	The Olmec civilization flourishes in south-central Mexico and along the Gulf Coast.
300 CE–900 CE	The Mayan civilization flourishes in the eastern portion of Mexico, especially the Yucatán.
900–1200 CE	The Toltec civilization flourishes in the Valley of Mexico.
1300	The Aztecs, seeking a permanent home, migrate into the Valley of Mexico, which is dominated by Tepanecs.
1325	Aztec island community of Tenochtitlán is founded in Lake Texcoco. The Aztecs become vassals and mercenaries of Tepanecs.
1375–1396	Acamapichtli is the first *tlatoani* of Tenochtitlán; Aztecs are no longer mercenaries.
1396–1417	Huitzilihuitl is the second *tlatoani.*
1417–1427	Chimalpopoca is the third *tlatoani.*
1427–1440	Itzcóatl is the fourth *tlatoani.*
1428	Aztecs join with Texcoco and Tlacopan to form the Triple Alliance; they defeat the Tepanacs and others, and create the Aztec Empire.
1440–1469	Montezuma I is the fifth *tlatoani.*
1450–1519	Aztecs fight "flower wars" with neighboring states Tlaxcala, Cholula, Huexotzinco, Tiliuhquitepec to gain sacrifice victims but no territory.
1469–1481	Axayacatl is the sixth *tlatoani.*
1481–1486	Tizoc is the seventh *tlatoani.*
1486–1502	Ahuitzotl is the eighth *tlatoani.*
1502–1520	Montezuma II is the ninth *tlatoani.*
1519	Spaniards under the command of Hernán Cortés land on Gulf Coast and make their way to Tenochtitlán, where they are greeted by and become guests of Montezuma II.
1520	Spanish troops under the command of Pedro de Alvarado massacre hundreds during a human sacrifice ceremony. The Aztecs attack and drive the Spanish from Tenochtitlán. Montezuma II is killed during the fighting. He is succeeded by Cuitláhuac, the tenth *tlatoani,* who shortly dies from smallpox.
1521	Cuauhtémoc is the eleventh *tlatoani.* Spanish and allies lay siege to Tenochtitlán. Smallpox epidemic decimates the Aztecs. Cuauhtémoc surrenders to Cortés on August 13. The Aztec Empire is no more.

CHAPTER NOTES

Chapter 1: Who Were the Aztecs?

1. David Carrasco and Scott Sessions, *Daily Life of the Aztecs: People of the Sun and Earth* (Westport, CT: Greenwood Press, 1998), p. 32.

Chapter 2: How Did Aztec Society Work?

1. Michael Smith, *The Aztecs* (Cambridge, Mass.: Blackwell Publishers, 1996), p. 46.

2. Friar Diego Durán, *The History of the Indies of New Spain,* translated by Doris Heyden (Norman: University of Oklahoma Press, 1999), pp. 209–210.

Chapter 3: What Was an Aztec Family Like?

1. Bernardino de Sahagún, *Florentine Codex: General History of the Things of New Spain,* translated and edited by Arthur J. O. Anderson and Charles E. Dibble (Salt Lake City: School of American Research and University of Utah, 1950–1982), Bk. VI: 90.

2. Friar Diego Durán, *Book of the Gods and Rites and the Ancient Calendar,* translated and edited by Fernando Horcasitas and Doris Heyden (Norman: University of Oklahoma Press, 1971), p. 122.

3. Miguel Leon-Portilla, *Aztec Thought and Culture: A Study of the Ancient Nahuatl Mind* (Norman: University of Oklahoma Press, 1963), p. 26.

4. Bernardino de Sahagún, *Florentine Codex,* Bk 8: 130.

5. Michael Smith, *The Aztecs* (Cambridge, Mass.: Blackwell Publishers, 1996), p. 118.

Chapter 4: What About Food, Feasting, and Fun?

1. J. Bayard Morris, editor and translator, *Five Letters of Cortés to the Emperor* (New York: W.W. Norton, 1962), pp. 87–89.

Chapter 5: What Was School Like?

1. M. Leon-Portilla, *Los Antiquos Mexicanos a traves de sus Cronicas y Canteras* (Mexico City: Fondo de Cultura Economica, Mexico City, 1961), p. 147; translated by Michael D. Coe and Rex Koontz, in *Mexico From the Olmecs to the Aztecs* (New York: Thames & Hudson, 2002), p. 193.

2. David Carrasco and Scott Sessions, *Daily Life of the Aztecs: People of the Sun and Earth* (Westport, Conn.: Greenwood Press, 1998), p. 109.

3. Bernardino de Sahagún, *Florentine Codex: General History of the Things of New Spain,* translated and edited by Arthur J. O. Anderson and Charles E. Dibble (Salt Lake City: School of American Research and University of Utah, 1950–1982), Bk. VI: 230–240.

4. Ibid., Bk. VI: 241–247.

Chapter 6: The Aztec Army and Making War

1. Friar Diego Durán, *Book of the Gods and Rites and the Ancient Calendar,* translated and edited by Fernando Horcasitas and Doris Heyden (Norman: University of Oklahoma Press, 2nd edition, 1977), cited in David Carrasco and

Scott Sessions, *Daily Life of the Aztecs: People of the Sun and Earth* (Westport, Conn.: Greenwood Press, 1998), p. 146.

Chapter 7: How Did They Create Art and Beauty?
1. Editors, Time-Life Books, *Aztecs: Reign of Blood and Splendor* (Alexandria, Va.: Time-Life Books, 1992), p. 127.
2. Michael Smith, *The Aztecs* (Cambridge, Mass.: Blackwell Publishers, 1996), p. 103.

Epilogue: The End of an Empire
1. Bernardino de Sahagún, *Florentine Codex: General History of the Things of New Spain,* translated and edited by Arthur J. O. Anderson and Charles E. Dibble (Salt Lake City: School of American Research and University of Utah, 1950–1982), Bk. 12:31.
2. Friar Diego Durán, *The History of New Spain* (translated by Doris Heyden, Norman: University of Oklahoma Press, 1994), p. 529.
3. Miguel Leon-Portilla, *The Broken Spears: The Aztec Account of the Conquest of Mexico* (Boston, MA: Beacon Press, 1962), pp. 92–93.

FURTHER READING

For Young Readers
Chrisp, Peter. *The Aztecs.* Austin, TX: Raintree Steck-Vaughn, 2000.
Lourie, Peter. *Hidden World of the Aztecs.* Honesdale, PA: Boyds Mill Press, 2006.
Shuter, Jane. *The Aztecs.* Chicago, IL: Reed Educational & Professional Publishing, 2002.
Sonneborn, Liz. *The Ancient Aztecs.* New York: Franklin Watts, 2005.
Stout, Mary. *Aztec.* Milwaukee: Gareth Stevens Publishing, 2004.

Works Consulted
Anderson, Arthur J.O., and Charles Dibble, translators and editors. *Florentine Codex: General History of Things of New Spain.* Salt Lake City: School of American Research and University of Utah, 1950–1982.
Aquilar-Moreno, Manuel. *Handbook to Life in the Aztec World.* New York: Facts on File, 2006.
Carrasco, David, Eduardo Matos-Moctezuma, and Scott Sessions. *Moctezuma's Mexico: Visions of the Aztec World.* Boulder, CO: University of Colorado Press, 2003.
Carrasco, David, and Scott Sessions. *Daily Life of the Aztecs: People of the Sun and Earth.* Westport CT, Greenwood Press, 1998.
Coe, Michael D., and Rex Koontz. *Mexico, From the Olmecs to the Aztecs,* fifth edition. New York: Thames and Hudson, 2002.

Editors, Time-Life Books. *Aztecs: Reign of Blood and Splendor.* Alexandria, VA: Time-Life Books, 1992.

Gruzinski, Serge. *The Aztecs, Rise and Fall of an Empire.* New York: H.N. Abrams, 1992.

Hassig, Ross. *Time, History and Belief: The Aztecs and Colonial Mexico.* Austin: University of Texas Press, 2001.

Heyden, Doris, translator. *The History of the Indies of New Spain.* Norman: University of Oklahoma Press, 1999.

Horcasitas, Fernando, and Doris Heyden, translators and editors. *Book of the Gods and Rites and the Ancient Calendar.* Norman: University of Oklahoma Press, 1971, 1977.

Konstam, Angus. *Historical Atlas of Exploration 1492-1600.* New York: Checkmark Books, 2000.

Leon-Portilla,, Miguel. *The Broken Spears: The Aztec Account of the Conquest of Mexico* (Boston, MA: Beacon Press, 1962).

Mann, Charles C. *1491: New Revelations of the Americas Before Columbus.* New York: A.A. Knopf, 2005.

Meyer, Michael C., William E. Beezley, editors. *The Oxford History of Mexico.* New York: Oxford University Press, 2000.

Phillips, Charles. *The Complete Illustrated History of the Aztec and Maya.* London: Hermes House, 2006.

Portilla, Miguel Leon, translator. *Aztec Thought and Culture: A Study of the Ancient Nahuatl Mind.* Norman: University of Oklahoma Press, 1963.

Salmoral, Manuel Lucena. *America 1492: Portrait of a Continent 500 Years Ago.* New York: Facts on File, 1990.

Shorris, Earl. *The Life and Times of Mexico.* New York: W.W. Norton, 2004.

Smith, Michael. *The Aztecs.* Cambridge, Mass.: Blackwell Publishers, 1996.

On the Internet

Fraser, Pamela. Aztec Culture, Children's Village of Sonoma County. http://www.kn.att.com/wired/fil/pages/listaztecspa.html

Jamail Center for Legal Research, University of Texas School of Law. Law in Mexico Before the Conquest. http://tarlton.law.utexas.edu/rare/aztec/

Multnomah County Library, Ancient & Classical Cultures http://www.multcolib.org/homework/anchsthc.html#aztec

University of California, Irvine. Realms of the Sacred in Daily Life: Early Written Records of Mesoamerica http://www.lib.uci.edu/libraries/exhibits/meso/sacred.html

Voorburg, René. Aztec Calendar. http://azteccalendar.com

Aztlán (ahs-TLAHN)—Mythical ancestral home of the Aztecs, somewhere in northern Mexico.

calmecac (KAHL-muh-kak)—Special temple schools for the sons and daughters of Aztec nobles.

calpolli (KAHL-pol-ee)—A neighborhood or geographic area similar to our borough or township.

chinampa (chin-YAHM-pah)—Ground plot for growing crops, built from swampy mud, piled above the water surface and spread flat.

cihuacoatl (sih-wah-koh-AA-tl)—The Aztec king's first assistant and principle adviser, usually the high priest.

conquistadores (kon-KISS-tuh-dor-ees)—Spanish for "conquerors," referring to Hernán Cortés and his men.

divine (duh-VYN)—Having a godlike presence, a supreme being, someone beyond human power and control.

glyph (GLIF)—Carved or inscribed or painted symbols of an idea or event.

Huitzilopochtli (hwee-tsil-oh-POH-tlee)—Aztec god of the sun and war.

maguey (muh-GAY)—Abundant cactus plant that provided hide and needles used in making Aztec commoner clothing.

mercenaries (MER-seh-nayr-eez)—Soldiers hired to fight for someone else.

obsidian (ob-SIH-dee-un) **glass**—Very sharp material formed from volcanic rock, which is found throughout the Valley of Mexico.

Pleiades (PLEE-uh-deez)—A bright constellation that Aztec priests watched during the New Fire ceremony.

Quetzalcoatl (ket-sal-koh-AA-tul)—The Aztec feathered serpent god of the morning and creation who was defeated and banished by the god of the night.

soothsayers (SOOTH-say-ers)—Aztec priests who claimed to foretell the future by consulting the stars and Aztec glyphs.

tamale (tah-MAH-lee)—Cornmeal dough that's filled with meat or beans and steam-cooked.

telpochcalli (tel-poh-KAH-lee)—"Youth houses"; general schools for sons and daughters of commoners.

Tenochtitlán (ten-ok-tit-LAHN)—The capital of the Aztec Empire, site of modern Mexico City.

Tlaloc (t-LAY-lok)—Aztec god of rain and harvest.

Tlatelolco (t-lat-el-OL-koh)—Location of the Aztec great market near Tenochtitlán.

tlatoani (t-lah-toh-AH-nee)—Nahuatl for an Aztec king or ruler.

tortilla (tor-TEE-ya)—A thin, flat bread made from ground corn.

tribute (TRIH-byoot)—Merchandise and raw materials paid periodically by conquered peoples and by commoners to nobles.

Valley of Mexico—The highlands plateau in central Mexico surrounded by mountains where Aztec society developed.

ABOUT THE AUTHOR

William Noble, who has been a freelance writer and teacher for thirty-five years, has more than twenty books and hundreds of articles and stories in print. Many of his works have been book-club selections, and he has spoken or taught at writers' conferences, colleges, and universities from coast to coast. A practicing attorney for seven years before devoting full time to writing, and a member of the Pennsylvania bar, he received his law degree from the University of Pennsylvania and his undergraduate degree in history from Lehigh University. He is a member of the Author's Guild and listed in Who's Who in America and Contemporary Authors.